Toward World Peace:

Seeing the Unity Between Us All

D1452972

By
Stephen Knapp

Dedicated to:
Everyone who has endeavored to
overlook our differences and see our similarities
to bring unity, peace and harmony into the world.
And to those who can see we are all the same.
After all:
What would there be without average people?
The only people that I could be.
What would there be without average people?
It seems there would be no place for me.

ISBN:0-9617410-5-8
Library of Congress Catalog Card Number:
97-062504

PUBLISHED BY

PROVIDING KNOWLEDGE
OF
REALITY DISTINGUISHED FROM ILLUSION
FOR THE WELFARE OF ALL

The World Relief Network
P. O. Box 15082
Detroit, MI 48215
U.S.A.

Other books by the author:
The Secret Teachings of the Vedas
The Universal Path to Enlightenment
The Vedic Prophecies: A New Look into the Future
Proof of Vedic Culture's Global Existence

CONTENTS

CHAPTER ONE

Seeing the Unity Between Us All

We all want a peaceful, happy life. We all want peace in the world. We all want to be treated fairly, to have the same opportunities to pursue life, liberty, and happiness. Even the *Declaration of Independence* of the United States, as established on July 4, 1776, specifically states: "We hold these truths to be self-evident, that all men are created equal, that they are endowed by their Creator with certain unalienable Rights, that among these are Life, Liberty and the pursuit of Happiness."

The United States is founded on the principle that all men are created equal and, thus, should be treated equally. This certainly is a premise that should promote a peaceful coexistence with one another. So why does it seem to be so difficult to achieve? Why do so many disturbances to the hope for peace develop on so many different levels? There are disagreements and quarrels between races, religions, countries, cultures, and even next door neighbors over minor differences. So what can we do about it?

First of all, there are five great enemies of peace which inhabit all of us: avarice, ambition, envy, anger, and pride. These also take shape in our passions, prejudices, vices, weaknesses, and our intellectual and spiritual ignorance. If these were removed, we would enjoy perpetual peace. However, these are not qualities found in relations between people. Rather, they are within ourselves, hampering our ability to relate. We not only have to work on problems that exist in our relations with others, but also on the problems that exist within us. So our primary enemies are inside us. Thus, in order to grow in our understanding of each other, it is first better to rid ourselves of these internal enemies than to inflict these characteristics out on others. After all, if we want to change the world, the change starts with ourselves.

FACTORS THAT KEEP US APART

One of the main concerns in establishing peace and harmony in this world is an old problem, mentioned in the Taoist text *Chuang Tzu* (11): "Men of this world all rejoice in others being like themselves, and object to others not being like themselves." One of the main reasons for this is that everyone acts under the influence of different bodily conceptions of life. This causes three of the above-mentioned enemies: envy, pride, and anger. Because of our bodily conception, we may become proud of who we are, envious of others, and angry over their apparent differences from us. Because of these diverse perceptions, people cannot act in harmony in this material world. To act in harmony and unity, there must be a central focus.

Since everyone is actually a spiritual being, a soul within the material body, accepting the body as oneself is an illusion. This illusion causes one to think "I am American," or "I am European," or "I am white," or black, or fat, or skinny. We may think this is my country, my family, my friends, my society, or my political party, and everyone else is different. What is this consciousness of being American or Russian? A Republican or Democrat? Black or white? It is all illusion based on the impermanent identity of the ever-changing body. It is the "I" and "My" consciousness. It creates a society in which people fight with each other because of the differences of the body and their identification with it. The whole world exists under this illusion. So how can there be peace? Even though government leaders talk about peace, and meet in peace conferences, there can be no peace as long as this false consciousness continues.

When people are under the bodily concept of life, they do not know that their real self-interest is spiritual. Therefore, they try to adjust things materially: changing their situation, changing their job, their government, their wife or husband, their living arrangement, or their neighborhood. They think such adjustments are the way to be happy and to improve their lives. These arrangements, however, are temporary. Sooner or later more changes will again be needed.

Furthermore, leaders are doing the same thing. They try to change things through political, economic, or military adjustments. However, more often than not, it is merely guesswork. The same problems, fighting, and antagonisms continue.

The United Nations in New York has been formed to try to calm this fighting so countries and people can work out their differences and work in unity. Instead, people often come together and blame or threaten each other. Unity has not been achieved. Actually, more flags are flying. More countries and borders have been established. Everyone has their own agenda. Disagreements between countries have increased. More countries want their own territory to do what they want and to keep others out because of mutual distrust or hatred. Just as Pakistan was formed for Muslims in an attempt to settle the fighting, there are also fights between the Catholics and Protestants in Britain, and similar fighting between religions, cultures, and tribes in many parts of the world. This brings the whole world into a deplorable state.

When we are in the bodily concept, seeing the differences between us, it is often the case that we feel our group, our class of people, our culture or religion, is the best. It is the nature of this sort of material consciousness to cause dissension and disagreement. Some people or group will always have a feeling of superiority. This gives rise to the feeling that they can encroach on the land, property, or rights of others who they may feel are not as worthy to do or have what they want. In such a case, how can there be peace or unity? However much people wish for peace or unity, false pride or too high an estimation of one's own values only takes human society away from peace.

Unless we have a central focus on the goal and identity of humanity, all talk of unity is merely utopian: It will never happen. As long as people act under the influence of thinking they are their bodies, born of a certain country, culture, religion, and loyal only to that particular identity, people will continue to fight like cats and dogs. No matter how much we desire peace between everyone so we can live in unity, as long as we are in this bodily concept of life peace is not possible.

The only possibility of unity is in rising above the bodily platform of life and coming to the spiritual platform. Then there is a genuine possibility of unity on this planet because we can focus on the real identity of humanity as the uniting force among us all.

* * *

The failure to control our minds and senses is a weakness which creates the internal enemies: our vices, avarice, and misguided ambitions. Everyone may want peace and unity, but if we think we are these bodies, then we think the goal of life is to satisfy our mind and senses. So everyone chases after different goals and objects to find pleasure and happiness. In the attempt to attain our goals and satisfy our desires, there are many things we feel we need to do or have, some of which are quite unnecessary. These often create more problems than they solve. Such activities create bad habits, misguided aims of life, which actually take away whatever peace of mind we are trying to find. Or we may want the same thing that others want. So due to competition, there may be much quarreling, fighting, and struggle, all over the same prize or position.

To try and satisfy our body and senses, we become mad after attaining money. Some people even reach the point of lowering themselves to engage in illegal, dangerous, or immoral pursuits for the acquisition of money. Although there is no lack of money in the world, there is a scarcity of peace because those who have money hoard it, simply to accumulate more of it. In many cases people do not use it for beneficial purposes, but only for selfish gratification. Peace can be attained when we all live simply, satisfied with only what we need without extravagances, using money for purposes that benefit others. Then, peace will not be a scarce commodity. There can be peace and prosperity in the world when there is a good and sane civilization.

Even in the wealthiest countries, many people are not enjoying real peace and unity. When society is overwhelmed by desires for gratifying their senses, whatever money is earned soon becomes spoiled or wasted on temporary thrills and trivial pursuits. Desires for pampering the senses lead one to lust, envy, jealousy, territorialism, and generally low consciousness. Individuals' failure to control their minds and senses in efforts to fulfill their desires can escalate to such desperate measures as robbery, rape, and even murder.

Material lust is like a blazing fire, never leaving a person with any peace. Such desires always force people to attempt to satisfy their cravings. The flames of such desires consume all hope for peace in such individuals. When society is made of many such individuals, whose primary interest is to simply satisfy their own desires and gratify their senses, this disorder prevents peace in human society. Society remains in a state of escalating chaos. Such disorder grows to the degree in which society pursues selfish gratification.

Without controlling our mind and senses, there is no possibility for peace. Only people who can give up their numerous material desires by spiritualizing their consciousness can attain real peace of mind and work in peace and unity with others.

As Krishna says in *Bhagavad-gita* (2.71): "A person who has given up all desires for sense gratification, who lives free from desires, who has given up all sense of proprietorship and is devoid of false ego--he alone can attain real peace."

And (*Bg*.2.70): "A person who is not disturbed by the incessant flow of desires--that enter like rivers into the ocean, which is ever being filled but is always still--can alone achieve peace, and not the man who strives to satisfy such desires."

When society is bent toward satisfying materialistic desires, displaying such desires through alcoholism, drug-taking, financial cheating, intrigue, and other frivolous activities, that is indicative of irreligiosity. When this is prevalent, it is not possible to stop the corresponding evils of corruption, lower moral standards, and nepotism. Legislation and police laws are not enough to stop such nefarious habits. Only advocacy of the principles of cleanliness, austerity, simple living, mercy and truthfulness, along with understanding genuine spiritual knowledge, can purify the consciousness of society. This alone can pave the way for a chance to establish real peace and unity.

* * *

The sense of false proprietorship is another of the major factors that keep us from attaining unity. For example, in a successful business everyone is working for the same result, producing a quality product and selling it to many people for a good profit. If the company functions properly, everyone is aware that the company and the profits belong to the proprietor. In that case, there can be peace. But if someone steals products, equipment, or money, thinking that it is their company, then there cannot be peace. It disrupts the whole company.

Similarly, only if we are aware that everything belongs to God, that He is allowing all of us to use the gifts of nature for our well-being, can there be peace and harmony. That is the consciousness that needs to be developed individually as well as globally. You may have much property or wealth, but as soon as you neglect to recognize that they are all the blessings of the Supreme, then you are under the influence of *maya*, illusion. Then you will sink to the bodily conception of life, thinking in terms of "I," "Me" and "Mine."

In the bodily concept we think, "This is mine. This belongs to me. You cannot enter my property, my culture, my religion. . ." In that mentality you become disturbed and create disturbances. Only a few hundred years ago the native American Indians were considered the proprietors of America and struggled against the invaders who wanted to be the new proprietors. Today, the Europeans and their descendants are claiming proprietorship. However, in another several hundred years perhaps someone else will be here to claim proprietorship. The land is here, but the people who live on it may change. So proprietorship is temporary, and another illusion. This false claim to be the proprietor of the earth, by so many factions of people, creates many disturbances on this planet.

Only in spiritual consciousness can there be the realization that portions of this planet do not belong to particular men. It belongs to God and we all belong to the Supreme. God is the supreme proprietor. Only by realizing this and acting in that consciousness can there be peace. The world leaders should especially understand this knowledge. If the world leaders understand this, then they may be able to lead society toward the proper changes to produce peace.

Due to the bodily concept of life, and the false sense of proprietorship, there is a huge misappropriation of money toward large and costly weapons for self-defense. In some ways these may be necessary. However, rather than bringing peace to the world, these weapons actually threaten to destroy society and the entire planet. Huge amounts of money, and the lives of many people, are wasted on experiments to develop powerful and ever more dreadful weapons. Of course, there is a need to defend oneself and prepare for attacks, but the whole world has gone crazy, threatening and counter-threatening each other. And huge amounts of money could be used instead for more important and beneficial ways to attain world peace. Some governments have diverted the profits from money producing enterprises to fund their military to the point where common citizens have to do without many otherwise affordable amenities. Thus, the productive energy of the human race is spoiled through this competition for military development.

The military of one country pursues technological superiority over some other country. However, the invention of new bombs and weapons means that people become more violent and more cruel, or more worried and paranoid. Thus, they spend their energy creating something that brings havoc and destruction to all. They say these weapons are meant to establish peace, but the leaders who engage in this endanger the lives of everyone.

It is not difficult to realize that the Supreme Being is the ultimate proprietor and owner of all planets. He is the owner of the land, sea, and air. That understanding cures our sense of false proprietorship. And because we are all spiritual parts and parcels of the Supreme Father, being His sons and daughters, we have the right to use our father's property. But we should not take the same right away from others. And we should not take more than we need. Only then is there the possibility of peace in the world and unity between us.

As Krishna states in the *Bhagavad-gita* (5.29): "A person in full consciousness of Me, knowing Me to be the ultimate beneficiary of all sacrifices and austerities, the Supreme Lord of all planets and demigods, and the benefactor and well-wisher of all living entities, attains peace from the pangs of material miseries."

The human race should take this wisdom and not quarrel over temporary material possessions. We should be satisfied with whatever we have been blessed with that is needed to survive in this world. Life is not often easy, but it becomes easier when we help each other to get through it. That is only possible when we work together.

HAVING SPIRITUAL VISION

A materialistic or godless society arises from illusion. This is caused by ignorance of our real, spiritual identity. The results of such a society are chaos and confusion, to quarrels and lamentation. In material consciousness we see that there are varieties of life and engagements, but there is little focus for a common goal. Everyone has their own views, their own goals. And everyone thinks their view is the best. However, in spiritual consciousness there can be many varieties and engagements, but the goal and focus are the same. That is to act in ways that are moral, peaceful, and in harmony with the Supreme. This is the way God will be pleased and the planet will be a pleasant place on which to live. That is the difference between material and spiritual consciousness. Thus, if we want to rid ourselves of illusion and establish unity among ourselves, we must focus on our spiritual identity.

CHAPTER TWO

Breaking Down the Barriers

As previously explained, in the materialistic state of consciousness one thinks, "I am an American or Russian, Catholic or Protestant, white or black. I am loyal to my country and countrymen. I work for my homeland. Everyone else is different." This type of consciousness is established in the individual to the degree to which he or she is in the bodily concept of life. The bodily concept of life, thinking one is the body, means to focus on these designations. But real life, seeing beyond the illusion that we are only bodies, is to be without designations. When we realize that we are all spiritual beings, that our souls are all the same in nature, character, quality and identity, then we will begin reaching a level of reality. This is the only way there can be any real unity between us all.

This whole world belongs to human society at large. Actually, everything belongs to the Supreme Being. We are all guests on this planet. Our time here is temporary. We may stay here for sixty, seventy, or a hundred years or so, and then we are forced out at the time of death. We are forced to give up our body, along with our family, friends, country, countrymen, our land, property, and whatever else is connected with this temporary body. So there is no need to feel that I belong only to one section of society or one family. We all go through the same basic pattern of life and have the same essential needs. We are all in this together. It takes everyone to make this planet work nicely. But when we think other than this, we create disunity and disharmony, which escalates to struggles, to fights, even wars between communities, cultures, and countries in various parts of the world. Then, there cannot be any peace.

9

In the highest levels of spiritual consciousness you reach a stage
in which you no longer react to the designations of the body. You see
beyond or through the body and recognize the spiritual identity of
each living being within the temporary physical vehicle. It is only
because of our bodies which keeps us all engaged in the effort to
survive. This effort does not need to be a reason for our separations
and quarrels. But it should be a reason why we all help each other get
through life in the material world.

WE ARE ALL WORKING TO ATTAIN THE SAME THINGS

When we look at each other from a bodily perspective we may
see how different we appear to be. However, when we take a closer
look, we can notice that we are all similar.

We are all working to attain things for our existence, such as a
peaceful life, a pleasant community in which to live, nice friends,
family, few worries or problems, food to eat, clothes to wear, shelter,
an education for our children, and good jobs which pay us fairly for
our work. We may have different jobs, different responsibilities, and
different backgrounds, but our needs and desires are not that
dissimilar. We are not very different from each other at all.

For example, the different parts of the body do different things,
and also look different. The head, arms, hands, legs, feet, and
stomach, all look and act differently. They have different functions.
However, they all work together to maintain the body and to feed the
stomach. By cooperating, they feel strong and happy. If the arms and
legs should question, "Why are we working so hard just to feed the
lazy stomach?" and they stop working, the whole body becomes
weak. The arms and legs also suffer. Therefore, because the arms and
legs belong to the body, they must also help maintain the body and,
thus, they help maintain themselves simultaneously. Similarly, we are
all part of the same planet. We all have the same essential goals. So
when we all work together to attain those goals, we are all helping
ourselves to reach a happy, pleasant life.

Another example of this is when a storm or tornado comes through a community and does extensive damage. This can actually help bring people together. Shortly before this writing, a tremendous storm ripped through the Detroit area. Houses were damaged, some were pulled off their foundations, trees and power lines were down. Streets were filled with debris and people were injured. Old people could not take care of themselves, others were running out of food. The only way the community could get back to a peaceful state of being was if the people all pulled together to clean up the streets and take care of those who were less well off and who needed attention. It did not matter who was black or white, Hispanic or Italian, old or young. Everyone needed to help each other. They were all in an emergency which required them to overlook whatever differences they may have. Otherwise, they could have all kept to themselves and suffered separately instead of helping each other get back to a normal existence. But is this what we need for us to break down the illusory differences between us to bring a community together? Do we need to get bonked on the heads by a storm to knock some sense into us regarding the need to work together, and that we are really not so different from each other? I should hope not. However, if such earth changes and emergencies bring about these sort of social conditions that bring society together, then there may be more of such occurrences.

The point is that not only do we all want the same things, but we are also vulnerable to the same fears, the same insecurities, the same loneliness, and the same need to feel appreciated, cared for, and loved. No one is above these anxieties, unless he or she is a rock. This is something else which we all have in common. And we can deal with them by ourselves, or we can admit these insecurities and discover that life is easier when we deal with them together.

SEEING THROUGH THE BODILY DISTINCTIONS

Regardless of what kind of body you have, or from what part of the world it originated, or what color it is, it is still nothing more than a temporary machine in which we are situated. It is a most amazing machine, but nonetheless, it is a bag of bones, muscles, and internal organs. And regardless of how beautiful your body may be, once the thin layer of skin is taken away, the sight will be enough to make most people want to run away. As the saying goes, beauty is only skin deep. This is not meant to demean the body. These bodies are valuable tools and much can be accomplished with them. However, everyday we need to feed it, clothe it, and bathe it. This is the same for all of us. Furthermore, once the soul leaves the body, the body no longer functions. It immediately begins to stiffen, break down, deteriorate, and produce foul odors. And yet, some people are so proud of their bodies.

Then when the body is dead, it is buried and gradually turns back into earth and the elements from which it was made. Or it is burned and turns into ashes. Or in some countries it is thrown out so the animals and birds can eat it, in which case the body turns into the stool of others. So for earth, ashes, or stool, we are taking so much care. For what reason? Because we are self-motivated and want to preserve ourselves, but the real self is within. We are the consciousness within the body.

So herein we can begin to understand that the body is merely the vehicle and it is not what gives a person his or her primary value. It is the character and qualities of the individual which makes a person. We have seen that even advanced scientists and philosophers who may be invalids, who are completely incapable of functioning properly on the physical level--now called physically challenged--may be held in great respect because of their scientific and intellectual abilities. In spite of their body, it is their mind and intellect for which they are known and appreciated, which shows that such things are more important than the body alone. Thus, calling them invalids, which means having no value, is obviously a completely inaccurate term.

Even movie stars who never show their true character on screen may be liked and appreciated by the public. But the public will want to know more about who such stars really are and will want to read about them and hear interviews with such actors and actresses. Only after knowing their real personality and character will the public love them for who they are and for more than their on-screen work.

The same goes for beautiful and talented models who, you could say, get paid large sums simply for their body. Their beauty may be appreciated by many, but only after their real personality and character is understood will they be loved with any depth. That is the same for anyone.

Regardless of what kind of body we have, it is only our physical covering. It is our character and personality which distinguishes us from others and gives us real value. We are more than these material forms in which we reside. So to judge someone simply by bodily distinctions is a shallow view of who we are. We have to look beyond the body to discover the real person. On a deeper level, we are all spiritual beings. That is what we all have in common. That should be the focus for establishing our unity. (Much more information on this is supplied in Chapter Three.)

BREAKING DOWN THE CULTURAL DISTINCTIONS

As we look back through history, there have been so many fights and wars between people of different cultures. There have been divisions drawn between Hindus and Muslims, Catholics and Protestants, Jews and Arabs, blacks and whites--the focal points of fierce battles. In this way, due to some feeling of patriotism to a country, idea, concept, or race, one may think that a certain group of people are "my people," or "my group or class," based on the relationship with the body and family and national traditions. However, as long as there is this feeling that those related to this body are "my kinsmen, my blood relatives, my countrymen," that everyone else is a foreigner, or inferior, that I do not care for those people; then there cannot be unity or peace in the world.

Based on bodily and cultural differences, there is so much fighting in which people are killed in the night of illusion. But without their temporary uniforms, they all look the same in the morning sunlight. So what is really the difference? It is only the mental conception of who we think we are. And because that is a mental conception, that means it can also change according to the mood of the flickering mind. The mind is always accepting this and rejecting that: This is good, that is bad. But these values also change according to the level of knowledge to which one is exposed. A person may think one way one day, and some other way the next. Then his or her ideals and values may change to something entirely different, and a person of one culture or religion may join that of another.

Of course, when we look around the world, we cannot deny that there are different types of religions, cultures, and traditions. You have Hinduism, Christianity, Islam, Buddhism, or the French culture, British, Irish, and Chinese. These have been established according to time, place, and people. It also makes the world more beautiful and interesting. They all have something to offer. It is not that we need to think that they are foreign or weird. There is meaning behind their traditions and practices. Many times while traveling in India I have seen tourists criticize some practice or tradition they see because they think it is strange. However, this mostly reveals their ignorance of what is happening and why. How can they get any understanding by merely watching and criticizing? They have to ask questions to learn the deeper meaning to the traditions. Otherwise, they may as well not have even gone to India. What is the point to see foreign customs, only to criticize and leave that country with strange impressions? Every culture has something to offer, but if you do not learn what it is, then what is the use of going there? If you do not know much about the culture, any culture, you do not have much to say about it.

How can we understand another person's culture when we are so full of judgments and opinions on how others should live? We may appreciate our own homeland, but we should also appreciate the ways of other people and the circumstances with which they must contend. Such understanding is what can dissolve cultural boundaries and prejudices.

The point is that each culture has different principles on the external or material platform, but by taking a deeper look at the meaning of the traditions and philosophy, we often find they are quite similar to our own, based on similar reasoning. They simply may be expressed in a different way. However, if we do not take the time to learn these internal meanings, the acts themselves will be forever misunderstood.

When we come to the spiritual platform of recognizing who we are, such differing external principles are very superficial. These varying customs are no longer considered as items of difference between us. We look past that. We take it in the same way a gardener sees how the difference of flowers add to the beauty of a garden. Sure, if you have one big garden with only one type of flower, it can be very pretty. But how much more beautiful is the garden when there are a variety of colorful flowers, each with its own color, design and fragrance? Furthermore, some flowers work better in different parts of the garden. Some flowers work better in shade than sun, and other flowers require less water. Many kinds of flowers work in different ways, but they work in harmony and unity to produce an inspiring garden. Similarly, the difference in cultures of the world add to the beauty, wisdom, and knowledge that we can share when viewed from this angle of vision. People of a particular culture may also be more accustomed or work better and more efficiently in certain parts of the world than others. They may also produce different fruits, crops, or products that are not produced in other parts of the world. So all cultures have something to contribute to allow that the world goes on nicely and efficiently. In this way, we should recognize that our differences are also our advantages. Therefore, all cultures around the world can work in harmony to make their contribution to the unity of the world. In this end, there is really no difference between any of us. Just as the Bible says in *Acts* (17.26), "God hath made of one blood all nations of men."

The fact is that it takes all kinds of people to make this world work. When everyone is working for the benefit of the world, everything can work smoothly, without conflicts, wars, and resentment. Only those with an unnecessarily high degree of attachment to their own bodies and cultures will feel condescendingly that other cultures are inferior, which creates a point of difference and disharmony between us. When one reaches spiritual consciousness, he rises above all of these limited considerations.

BREAKING DOWN THE RELIGIOUS DIFFERENCES

One of the most difficult of all things is to break down the barriers between us that have been caused by our religions. Religion is supposed to bring us closer to God, which should certainly uplift us and show us that we are all spiritual beings. In that way we are united. We can have a central focus. However, this is not how it has gone. This is mostly because each religion implies, or comes right out and says, that it is the best or the only way to God. All others are inferior and should be ignored, dominated, pushed away, or even destroyed by force.

A first-class religion is not the one that claims it is the highest religion. The first-class religion is that which teaches or trains one perfectly how to love God. That is first-class. And in such a first-class religion, no one will claim to be better than any other. That is because he or she will naturally see that we all have the same Supreme Father. The only difference between any of us is in the level of spiritual understanding we have, and how united we are to the Supreme Being. Otherwise, spiritually we are all the same, and whatever our bodily situation may be is temporary.

If you feel that your religion is the best of all others, it is natural to be loyal or appreciate what it has done for you. However, if you feel *superior* to others because of being a Muslim, or Christian, or something, then that is where your religion has failed. For you to feel that way means that it has provided you with incomplete knowledge. You have not made much spiritual advancement. If your religion has failed to bring you to the spiritual platform in which you can see the spiritual similarities between you and all other creatures, regardless of caste, creed, culture, or species, then your religion has failed. Or you have failed to follow it properly, or to its ultimate goal. It may have brought you to the path of being pious, but it has not brought you to the point of true love of God and spiritual vision. Real love of God includes the spiritual love for all others, without prejudice, bias, or condescending attitudes. If you have not attained this level, then you still have much progress to make either in your own religion or by adding the help of another more complete source of spiritual knowledge. Those who are not understanding in this way and criticize different systems of religion due to jealousy, envy, malice, or a sense of superiority, are simply revealing themselves to be very immature. They do not cherish love toward their own God, but show more regard for vain quarrels and contentions.

In *Ashoka's Edicts* it is rightfully stated, "Never think or say your religion is the best. Never denounce the religion of others. But honor in them whatever is worthy of honor." After all, what good is a religion which condemns everybody else's philosophy or symbols for God except its own? Some religions say that if God is represented in a form, beautiful or symbolic, or is established in a Deity, then it is heathen or superstition, so it is bad. But if God comes in the form of a dove, burning bush, or a pillar of fire, it is holy. This is completely contradictory to the understanding of the omnipotent ability of the Supreme.

In all religions throughout the world, the external differences are easily noticed. These may be in regard to rituals, posture, clothing, food, behavior, or sanctity. There will be differences in conceptions of God and the objects of worship, or in the name of God because of differences in language or traditions. So it is natural that religions of the world may become disunited because of these differences. But it is very improper that there should be quarrel among them on the grounds of this disunion. We should, as mature servants of God, think that the religion of others still holds the same worship of the same Highest Entity as my religion, my God. Their practice may be different and I may not understand it, so I appreciate my own religion. However, there is only one God, therefore I also respect this form of worship and offer my prayers to God who is being worshipped in a different way.

For example, the Jewish tradition has always implied that a Jewish soul has an advantage over non-Jews to realize or love God, but Judaism itself provides evidence to indicate otherwise. One quote that affirms that anyone has the ability to realize God, regardless of his race, religion, or sex, is: "Elijah said, 'I bring heaven and earth to bear witness that any human being, Jew or Gentile, man or woman, freeman or slave, according to his deeds, can become worthy of

Rauch HaKodesh, the Holy Spirit, the transcendental experience."
(*Tana DeBei Eliahu Rabba 9, Bahir II. 94*)

God does not favor one sect or religion over another, but monitor's one's sincerity, devotion, surrender, and willingness to help and love others. And God reciprocates with one to the same degree of his or her devotion and sincerity. God is not the kind of being who favors only one sect and allows all others to be damned. Everyone is a part of God, otherwise they would not be here, and He cares for all.

In order to show His concern, God sends not just one but as many messengers and representatives as it takes to help guide and deliver all beings from material existence. The essence of that message, and all genuine religion, is the same. They all teach that we should not get stuck in material life, but to keep moving toward pure spiritual existence. The essential method in all religions by which this is accomplished is simple: Love God, love all others as parts of God, and act in that way at all times. The Supreme Being has made it simple. It is only humanity that has created the confusion found in the divisions of religions.

From this it is clear that God is the Lord of all beings, and in many ways. God is a multi-faceted being, unlimited in knowledge, ability, character, and personality. If a person is so narrow that he or she can hold allegiance to one faith while condemning all others, he or she will understand God only through that way. They will not know, nor will they be able to understand, that they can realize different aspects of God through other religions or spiritual paths. It is often seen that the most fundamental religions are the most limited in their understanding of God, and also carry with it the extra luggage of prejudice and condemnation of all other religions and cultures. It goes back to the principle that people who know the least about something are also the most fearful about what they do not understand.

Only religionists who are inexperienced and not conversant with spiritual Truth consider their ways as good and superior while hating the ways of others. They may even destroy the temples and images of God of other religions. Thus, they actually show their hatred of God. All good men will refrain from such actions, and all those who engage in such deeds show their improper and animalistic mentality.

However, those religions with real faults--such as being atheistic, materialistic, rejecting the soul or the existence of the Supreme, or using evil methods in its worship--should not be regarded as genuine religions. Their doctrines are antagonistic to true spiritual love and can never please the Supreme Being.

We also need to understand that there is no such thing as two Supreme Beings, or a God of one religion and a God of another. Such distinctions are made through ignorance. God is one. The Absolute Truth is one. So how can there be two religions? When followers of different religions quarrel about Truth, it is a sign that they have yet to experience Truth. Rather than seeking an experience of the Truth, they spend their time in quarrels, nurturing their prejudices against others. They are still far away from God. The word *religion* comes from the Latin *religio*, which means to bind to God. If a religion does not teach how to directly link with God, to love, respect, and have regard for all others as His parts and parcels, then it can hardly be called religion.

Once again, God is one. There cannot be two. If there is another, then there is competition. And the one God is neither Hindu, Muslim, Christian, or anything else. Such classifications relate only in the way God is worshipped. Real religion does not mean that we stamp this person a Christian, someone else a Muslim, or Hindu, or a Jain. Such designations are names that have nothing to do with the reality of the soul. Unity between us will never be established by emphasizing such designations on the material platform. So if God is one, why should there be quarrels between those who worship the one God in different ways? There should be no such quarrels, unless they think they are worshipping a different God and feel their God is superior to the God of others. Such a mentality is childish.

Religion means to understand God and to abide by His laws. It means to understand the nature of the soul, which is to love and be loved, and to serve the ultimate lovable object, the Supreme Lover-- God. In this way, every living being is a servant of the Supreme Being. Religion means to understand that God is great. We are subordinate. It means to understand that God is the greatest friend and proprietor. He takes care of us. Furthermore, the ultimate purpose of religion is to regain your love for God and to return to God. This means you rise above earthly desires and designations and transcend material life. This is the real unity and purpose of life that we all share. Based on this essential principle, we should all serve, understand and love God. There is no difference. We may pursue different religions, but that is diversity in unity because we all worship the same God. When we realize that, then there can be peace and harmony.

Another way of looking at our unity is in the concept described in the *Vedas* that explain that one form of the Lord is the universe. We all exist within this universal form of God. None of us are disconnected from Him. Furthermore, none of us are disconnected from each other. Each and every one of us has a particular function in relation to the universal form of God. Although each one of us may have different responsibilities, nonetheless, carrying out our functions within this world in relation to the universal form of God gives unity and harmony between all living beings throughout the world. However, the disruption of discharging our spiritual nature is the cause of disharmony between the living beings. So in order to achieve real peace and unity, we should recognize the fact that everything in this world and everyone is a part of this universal form of the Lord. Everything is an expansion of the Supreme's energy. No one is independent. Everyone and everything is connected. There are many diverse manifestations of God's energy. And although our bodies may not all look and act the same, we are all one in the Supreme's universal form. This is unity in diversity. When life is based on living in this truth by understanding the universal nature of the Supreme and His creation, then embracing universal love and compassion is a normal state of being.

This unity in diversity can be seen in observing the essence of any culture or religion. What we first notice are the superficialities, such as the dress, the outward formalities, the customs, rituals, and festivals. But deeper than this we find the basis of the culture's origin, the history of its development, the explanation of its philosophy, and the meaning and purpose of its rituals and customs. Still deeper is the essence and goal of the religion. As already pointed out, that essence is based on the principle that the follower should learn and engage in the process of serving, glorifying, and loving the Supreme Being. So, on the essential platform, there is really not much that differentiates the ultimate goals of the world's major religions. The only difference in the authentic religions is the time in history in which they appeared, the place where they existed, and the people who were taught. But due to these factors there may be lesser or greater differences in doctrines, beliefs, and rituals. And depending on the intellectual ability of the people who were taught, there may be more or less spiritual knowledge that was provided. Thus, there are different levels of scripture. Some are more direct and complete than others in the same way an unabridged dictionary is more complete than one that is abridged; though they both contain the same type of information. So once again we find the basis of unity in diversity.

The most important difference, however, is the depth of philosophical understanding and spiritual knowledge each particular religious process has to offer, and the level of spiritual realization the aspirant can attain by following the process. It is a fact that all true religious paths can lead to God, but such deep experience is beyond the grasp of fundamental and materially motivated religions that are based on national or cultural traditions and feelings of superiority because of race or geographical region. Such religions fail in their attempts to promote universal or spiritual brotherhood because they lack the spiritual knowledge and potency necessary to do so. Furthermore, because of this deficiency, they cannot give their followers the process that will enable them to become fully spiritually realized. So they remain biased against others because they cannot rise above the materialistic vision that causes them to focus on superficial differences, such as race, creed, cultural background, sex, or dress.

So how do we solve this problem that keeps people of different religions or cultures from accepting each other and working together? It is both easy and difficult. The easy part is to understand that the people merely have to be willing to share their spiritual knowledge with each other. They can all keep their own traditions, holidays, festivals, and rituals, but the essential knowledge and science of the individual souls, the Supreme Soul, and the relationship between them is what is important and what can be easily shared. This spiritual science is not explained more thoroughly than in the Vedic literature (as has been summarized in one of my previous books, *The Secret Teachings of the Vedas*). In fact, comprehending this knowledge of the Absolute Truth is necessary for everyone's spiritual advancement, regardless of which spiritual process one is inclined to accept. There must be this kind of open and respectful exchange across global and cultural boundaries in order for peace and unity between all societies to exist. The hard part is to get people to agree to do this. But in some cases you have to look at other cultures and their philosophical systems to get answers that are not provided elsewhere.

In fact, the Bible agrees with the idea of researching other scripture for answers. In *II Timothy* (3.16-17) we find the following quote: "All scripture is given by inspiration of God, and is profitable for doctrine, for reproof, for correction, for instruction in righteousness, that the man of God may be perfect, thoroughly furnished in all good works." Therefore, it is without a doubt that all scripture everywhere is meant to uplift our consciousness. Such being the case, it is not contradictory to see similarities in various scriptures and spiritual cultures, and it actually adds to and proves the glory of God amongst all nations. The following quote elaborates on this point:

Know ye not that there are more nations than one? Know ye not that I, the Lord your God, have created all men, and that I remember those who are upon the isles of the sea; and that I rule in the heavens above and in the earth beneath; and I bring forth My word unto the children of men, yea, even upon all the nations of the earth? . . . Wherefore, because that ye have a Bible ye need not suppose that it contains all My words; neither need ye suppose that I have not caused more to be written. For I command all men, both in the east and in the west, and in the north and in the south, and in the islands of the sea, that they shall write the words which I speak unto them; for out of the books which shall be written I will judge the world, every man according to their works, according to that which is written. (*Book of Mormon, 2 Nephi*, 29.7, 10-11)

The above quote is not unlike the Bible verse in *Romans* (10.12-13): "For there is no difference between the Jew and the Greek: for the same Lord over all is rich unto all that call upon him. For whosoever shall call upon the name of the Lord shall be saved."

We herewith have the reasoning why all our petty quarrels, whether between Catholics and Protestants, Hindus and Muslims, nation and nation, are nothing more than a sign of our ignorance and animalistic tendencies which actually disqualify us from making any spiritual advancement. We may think we are a chosen people, but if we have no spiritual vision to see the unity between all people, then the "promised land" is a lot farther away than we think. For God remembers all of us and, indeed, supplies all nations the knowledge by which they can spiritually advance and live peacefully, depending on their ability to understand and use it. After all, those who are sincerely trying to advance are all sons of God, as verified in *Romans* (8.14): "For as many as are led by the spirit of God, they are the sons of God." A similar statement is in *John* (1.12): "But as many as received him, to them gave he the power to become the sons of God, even to them that believe on his name." Thus, we are all God's children, as also confirmed by Lord Krishna in *Bhagavad-gita* (9.17-18) in which He says that He is the father of the universe, the mother, the grandfather, the object of knowledge, the purifier, the sacred *om*, and the *Rig, Sama,* and *Yajur Vedas*. He is the goal, the support, the master, the witness, the abode, and the most dear friend. Krishna also says (*Bg*.7.6) that He is the origin and dissolution of the entire universe, and (*Bg*.4.35) by knowing the Truth you will see that all beings are a part of Him and belong to Him. Thus, by understanding how we are all spiritually related, all sincere souls will find no difficulty in harmoniously working together and helping one another to understand the laws of the Supreme and advance accordingly, whether we are brother and brother, or nation and nation.

So if we are all spiritually related and can find similarities in the basic law of all religions, then what is the difficulty in cooperating with each other within the essential principles of all religions? And what is the essential principle we are all meant to follow? The essence of the law, as found in the Vedic, the Judaic, the Christian, the

Islamic, and other cultures, instructs us to surrender to God and work together to please Him according to His instructions. For example, when the Pharisees asked Jesus which was the great commandment in the law, he told them: "Thou shalt love the Lord thy God with all thy heart and with all thy soul, and with all thy mind. This is the first and great commandment." (*Matthew* 22.37-38) Lord Krishna taught the same thing in *Bhagavad-gita*: "Always think of Me and become My devotee. Worship Me and offer your homage unto Me. Thus you will come to Me without fail. Abandon all varieties of religion and just surrender unto Me. I shall protect you from all sinful reaction. Do not fear." (*Bg.*18.65-66)

In the *Koran* (9.112) we find it said that those who turn to God in repentance and serve and praise Him, and engage in devotion to God, who bow down and pray, who do good and avoid evil, will rejoice. So proclaim these glad tidings to the believers. We also find it said (19.65) that everyone should worship the Lord of the heavens and the earth and be patient in constant worship. For who is worthy of the same name as God?

In Zoroastrianism it is believed that a person must live according to the religious tenets if one hopes to joyfully go before the Creator in the next world. The best of all practices is the worship of God, for all are servants of God. So one must lead a righteous life since it is one's thoughts, words, and deeds that determine one's next life after death. Similarly, in Sikhism we find the precept that a true follower serves the Supreme Soul alone.

All of this information makes it clear that regardless of which religious system you choose, they all have the same purpose, and they all give the same principles. In this way, they are all united in their essential goals, the most important of which is to bring the living beings to the stage of cooperation in love of God. Obviously, our love for God will be shown by how much we cooperate with one another.

Unfortunately, before we reach this advanced stage we are in the lower levels of understanding. This immature level of love can take on the characteristics of a blind and fanatical allegiance to a particular process of religious expression rather than attachment to real love for God. In this situation, one may proudly and unnecessarily feel that he is on the highest path, and then will denounce every other process and culture without the proper spiritual understanding of himself or others. This is nothing more than sentimentality and fanaticism. Real love of God, which also displays love for all other living beings, will not develop within a person if he or she harbors such a divisive mentality. *People who show their love for their own religion by hating all others will spiritually stagnate and cause disharmony and quarrels between those of their religion and those of others.* Someone may be a kind, generous, and devout person amongst those of his own culture, while ready to howl, insult, hate, and do injury to those of another. This is love of the lowest level, similar to the way a dog may love its master and will show it by snarling at anyone else. Only those individuals and dry forms of religion that are bereft of real spiritual knowledge look at all others with hate and suspicion.

Only when one's consciousness becomes mature does this form of fanaticism or immature enthusiasm subside. Then real love and respect for all will naturally emanate from that person. As one becomes closer to the all-loving Supreme Being by the development of his own love for God, no longer can he be an instrument of hatred or prejudice because he sees everyone equally with spiritual vision. Thus, he walks away from the animalistic quarrels and wars that others take so seriously due to their ignorance of spiritual reality.

We have to remember that we are in this world but not of it. We are all spiritual beings who are temporarily residing in the material creation. It is futile to try and make a permanent home here, or attempt to be fully content and happy by being absorbed in material pleasures. This world does not and never will offer that kind of accommodation. A spiritual being in the material world, which is what we all are, is like a fish out of water: It is an incompatible situation. So we must understand the reality of our circumstance, that we are all transients evolving in a temporary situation on our way from one point of existence to another. So what is this life? It is nothing more than a moment on our great path towards full enlightenment. The world primarily is a field for activity which we can use to evolve to a higher state of being, and the body is the tool or vehicle in which we engage in those acts. But if we forget that, then we get caught in the illusion that this world is the cause and basis of our happiness, and our temporary body is the basis of our identity. Nothing can be further from the truth, and anyone with some proper understanding will see this.

By uplifting our consciousness, one will realize his or her spiritual identity and know that the immaterial realm pervades everything within as well as outside this material creation. Therefore, one who has become evolved and detached from the material focus of life knows that he is a spiritual being and a part of the divine strata. In this sense, wherever he goes, he is already home. A person who lives in this consciousness knows that there are only three things that are eternal: (1) the Supreme Being, (2) all the individual spiritual entities, and (3) the relationship between them, which is based on divine love. This spiritual love is all that has to be reawakened. This is the real goal of life. The spiritual strata, or fully enlightened consciousness, is where that love can manifest to the fullest degree.

If somehow or other the people of the world could give up their superficial differences and join together in genuine spiritual activity, the consciousness of society in general could change to such a degree that this very planet could become spiritually surcharged. It is not that we have to work for a specific change to bring about solutions to the world's problems, but when the consciousness of the people becomes purified, the solutions to the problems will become obvious and the necessary changes will automatically begin to manifest. The process starts from within, as the Bible states: "And when he (Jesus) was demanded of the Pharisees, when the kingdom of God should come, he answered them and said, The kingdom of God cometh not with observation: Neither shall they say, Lo here! or, Lo there! for, behold, the kingdom of God is within you." (*Luke* 17.20-21) Therefore, entering the spiritual realm, or changing the world in which we presently live, is simply a matter of reawakening our dormant divine consciousness. It is not a matter of outward observation, but it is an inward process of transformation and development.

If the people of the world would be more inclined to recognize that spiritual advancement is a process of inner transformation and participate in this process, and share with each other the different levels of higher knowledge from other cultures rather than merely accepting one particular religious dogma and rejecting all other forms of spiritual growth, then it becomes possible for all of humanity to be a united people. After all, a true religion respects whatever level of universal truth is found in any other culture and religion. Everyone could band together with a common cause of helping each other become enlightened: A universal religion based on hearing about and glorifying the Supreme. Every religion does this, so why not do it together? The only difference then would be whether people were theists or atheists, and atheists are simply those who have no spiritual experience or cannot fathom the depths of divine knowledge.

Otherwise, a world full of isolated religious cultures and doctrines is a world full of scattered and incomplete portions of the universal path to the Absolute Truth. Thus, we must seek to unite these paths by finding the common source from which these portions have sprung, as I have tried to point out in my other books, *The Secret Teachings of the Vedas*, and *The Universal Path to Enlightenment*. When you find that source, you will find the doorway that leads to full realization of the Absolute Truth and the clear consciousness through which we can see that all living beings share the same immaterial identity. Spiritually we are all one family. And on this level of consciousness it becomes obvious that all temporary material differences are superficialities. It is only people's own immature prejudice, caused by their spiritual ignorance, that stop people of the world from being united and cooperating together. Remembering that God is in everyone, and everyone is here by the will of God, and that God cares for all beings, you can respect anyone.

FOCUSING ON THESE DISTINCTIONS MEANS ANIMAL CONSCIOUSNESS

In animal life, there are more birds and insects than human beings on the planet. And, although there may be difficult times for the animals, there are no threats of wars, economic sanctions, political upheaval, massacres based on cultural cleansing, or slavery. So in animal life there is still some peace. However, in human life, you will find war, racial tensions, and economic instability. You also find political problems, industrial pollution, environmental hazards, and many other problems in society that animals do not have or do not cause. This is because people have missed the true goal of life, which is to develop their spiritual consciousness. Because of this, in some ways human life now has lost the simple peace that is found in ordinary animal life. So in some ways, in spite of our technological advancement, you could say that because of the misdirected aim of life humans have descended lower than the animals. However, there is more to this than simply reflecting on our social conditions.

Let us put this consciousness in perspective. According to the Vedic literature, there are many millions of huge universes scattered throughout the material creation. In each universe are many galaxies which contain innumerable stars and planets. In one galaxy is our solar system which is a tiny speck within the galaxy. In our solar system are several large planets. Our planet earth is just one of those planets, with several large continents. Many millions of people are on each continent. On one continent is the United States, which has many large cities. In one large city there are many streets and office buildings. Each office building has hundreds of people and many rooms. However, in one large office building there is one room in particular which has a man behind his desk, thinking that he is very important. He thinks the world depends on him. In reality, he is like a tiny speck of dust in the universe, which can easily go on without him. This attitude of importance, or of snooty, self-imposed superiority, which often leads to the condescending criticism of others because of bodily designations, is due to the bodily concept of life: Animal consciousness. This slow, unprogressive mentality prevents society from developing to the heights of advanced societal evolution. It keeps people bound to the lower levels of viewing themselves.

Those who are in the bodily concept of life, who see the bodily designations such as race, creed, nationality, tradition, sex, or age, have lower consciousness. They may think something like this: "I am a white, American, middle-aged Christian. And here is another white,

American, Christian of European descent, he is my friend. And there is a big, black man who follows his African ways. He is different, he is not my friend. I will avoid him." Or someone else may be thinking he is German, English, or Japanese, or Buddhist, Muslim, or Jain, and base all of their views from that perspective. Such people who think like this have an animalistic consciousness. Why? Because dogs and cats react in the same way. Some dog sees a cat and reacts to it as if it is thinking, "There is a cat, my enemy, so let me run and bark and chase it away or fight with it. And there is a rabbit, food, so let me try to catch it and eat it. Then I will enjoy. And there are other dogs, so let me go see them and we can all run and bark at smaller dogs, or bark at people or cars that drive by." Cats also react to different animals in the same way. A cat may see a dog and instinctively run away, trying not to be seen. Or the cat may see a mouse and run after it to catch and eat it. Or it may react to a female cat to go see what it can do with her. This is a very simple example, however, this is what dogs and cats do. The point is that if a dog reacts to stimuli in this way due to the type of body it has, and if I am thinking I am a white American because I was born in a white body on American soil, or an African because I have a black body, then how is my consciousness different from the dog's? So the bodily conception of life is practically the same as animal consciousness.

People reveal their animalistic consciousness by the critical words they speak about others. Such attitudes and the slighting comments people make based on this consciousness is also how such people reveal themselves to be slow-minded, backwards, and absorbed in animal vision.

"Both animals and men share the activities of eating, sleeping, mating and defending. But the special property of the humans is that they are able to engage in spiritual life. Therefore, without spiritual life, humans are on the same level as animals." (*Hitopadesh*)

The Vedic philosophy of the East explains that people who do not realize they are the spirit soul within the material body can hardly be considered as human beings. They are still like animals until they understand their spiritual identity. Those, however, who know they are the spiritual being inside the body can consider themselves to be humans. Only on that platform can there be some actual unity between us. But there will never be any unity between us when we are thinking of our bodily differences; such as being a German Protestant, an Italian Catholic, or an Indian Hindu. As long as people think in this animalistic, bodily concept, there can be a hundred United Nations and still the threat of quarrels and wars will not be reduced. It is not possible. If you bring in rulers of countries that think in this bodily concept, there may be so many talks, but no unity. It is hardly any different than to bring in a dozen dogs and request them to live peacefully. No, they will not live peacefully. They will continue to bark and fight over position, territory, food, and females. In other words, as long as you keep such leaders who think in this way, how can there be any possibility of change? And if the leaders think this way, the common people will, too.

In spite of all our advancement and education, if people continue to deal with each other like cats and dogs, peace cannot be attained. Only by developing our spiritual consciousness can there be peace. Therefore, the consciousness has to be raised to the level of human beings, and human life begins only when one understands that he or she is not this body but the spirit soul within.

The only way for all of us to bring unity and harmony amongst ourselves and, thus, bring peace to the planet is to help spread that knowledge which allows us to realize that we are not these bodies. The ancient Vedic texts of India, such as the *Bhagavat Purana* (11.23.59), explain that it is only due to our ignorance and mental confusion from the bodily concept of life that makes the soul perceive others as friends, enemies, or neutral parties. This confusion and ignorance is what needs to be corrected.

The point is that as long as we remain in the bodily concept, misidentifying ourselves as the body, there will not be any permanent unity between us. Only by understanding that we are not these bodies, that we are the spirit soul within, then unity between us, along with equality, fraternity, justice, and happiness, is possible. Only on the spiritual platform is it possible to attain unity and harmony between us, which can then pave the way for real peace in the world.

CHAPTER THREE

You Are Not Your Body

We need to rise above the bodily platform if we ever expect to reach a stage of permanent peace and unity. Even on an individual basis, real peace of mind can be attained only when one realizes that he or she is not the body. Otherwise, when you think you are your body you engage in the never-ending game of trying to satisfy your mind and senses, which always want new things for stimulation. The more you try to satisfy your senses, the more you will come under the control of lust, greed and anger. Lust is there when you want to satisfy your material desires. Greed is there when you want more than you need. Anger will always be there in some form when you fail to achieve what you want, or when you attain it but then lose it. The unmerciful masters of lust, greed and anger will never leave you alone. The only way you can achieve real peace of mind is by being free from your material desires, or at least most of them. That can only be possible when you realize you are not your body.

Happiness based on the body is like the pleasure a person feels when he or she drinks a tingling soft drink. As long as there is tingle on the tongue, there is some pleasure. The pleasure is gone when the sensation stops. So in material life, we may feel some pleasure or happiness during a thrilling or stimulating experience, or when we forget whatever problems or troubles we may have.

We all know there can be many problems and concerns in life, and forgetting these problems can also be a form of happiness. To help reach this forgetfulness one may engage in the drinking of alcoholic beverages, taking drugs, or other diversionary activities. These can bring on a state of temporarily forgetting one's problems, weaknesses, suffering, or fears. If people resort too much to these forms of escape, however, their problems may actually increase. This is false happiness. It is temporary. It does not cure any problems. The problems are still there when you come down from being high. So trying to satisfy the mind and senses in this way is not a means to real happiness. It is mostly a crutch to help get through life. Beyond that, these activities are frequently a cry for help.

Actually, identifying with the material body means suffering. There are so many temporary things we are forced to work for to satisfy the desires we have in our bodily concept of life. However, as soon as you realize that you are not your body, you can immediately become very jolly because you now have so many desires, goals and prizes for which you no longer need to struggle. That is because you have a clearer sense of what is relevant to your true happiness and real identity. In the material situation, we are always hankering for what we want and lamenting for what we have lost. This is anxiety. We suffer this way because we are always trying to possess that which is temporary. We may have something for a while, but then it is subject to wearing out, getting lost, or being taken away. Even when you approach a large, luxurious house of a wealthy person, there may be big fences and gates to keep others out, or a sign that warns "No Trespassers" or "Beware of Dog." This means that they may be so comfortable, but they are still in anxiety that someone will come and try to rob them and take away what they have.

So through our bodily conception of life, we are always hankering after material enjoyment and, therefore, trying to acquire and hold on to so many things in hopes of maintaining that enjoyment. The thought of losing our so-called valuables and what we cherish gives us great anxiety. So how can there be peace? Material happiness and anxiety are two sides of the same coin. They are superficial to the soul since they are essentially states of mind. In other words, it is only due to the mind's interactions with sense objects that determine the mind's pleasure, pain, or anxiety. The spirit soul is actually above such miseries and temporary pleasures.

One of the ancient Vedic texts of India, the *Srimad-Bhagavatam*, explains it this way: "O my Lord, the material miseries are without factual existence for the soul. Yet as long as the conditioned soul sees the body as meant for sense enjoyment, he cannot get out of the entanglement of material miseries, being influenced by Your external energy." (*Bhag*.3.9.9)

The miseries of life are caused only by the influence of the illusory energy which the living beings are subjected to as long as they refuse to understand their real identity. This is also confirmed in *Srimad-Bhagavatam*: "O my Lord, the people of the world are embarrassed by all material anxieties--they are always afraid. They always try to protect wealth, body, and friends, they are filled with lamentation and unlawful desires and paraphernalia, and they avariciously base their undertakings on the perishable conceptions of 'I' and 'mine.' As long as they do not take shelter of You, they are full of such anxieties." (*Bhag*.3.9.6)

The Vedic literature explains that working so hard for that which is temporary is like working hard for nothing at all. One day you may have what you have wanted. Another day it is gone. That is the nature of material objects and whatever happiness they provide. However, once you realize you are not your body, you become free from this anxiety. You become free to the degree to which you realize that, as a spiritual being, real happiness is not dependent on material objects and pleasures. If we want peace without anxiety, we must come to the spiritual position.

OUR REAL IDENTITY

We are the spirit soul inside the body. In this body we are covered by two layers: One is the subtle body, the other is the physical body. The subtle body is the mind, intelligence, and false ego. It is within this subtle body where all of our concepts of life and desires exist. The psychic activities, such as our thinking, willing, and feeling, take place within the subtle body. The false ego is the subtle element which makes us feel that we are this body, and that we are a certain kind of body, such as white, black, American, or European. Real ego means to understand that "I am," or "I am a spiritual being." False ego means that you think you are the temporary material body. The sense of designations comes from the false ego. The second and outer layer which covers the soul is the physical body, which holds all of our internal organs, muscles, nerves, and bones. These are made of blood, mucus, and skin, but are essentially made of different combinations of the common material elements of earth, air, fire, water, and ether. Combinations of all these elements, both physical and subtle, make the multi-dimensional vehicle or container in which we presently reside.

Those who are content simply to pamper and provide comforts for this container or body are materialists. Their consideration for happiness is the body. That is the general purpose of the material world. Beyond that, some people want to satisfy the mind through various arts, or philosophy. But both mental and physical happiness are considered external, and temporary, because they exist only within the realm of the material or subtle body and do not touch the spirit soul. It is like taking care of the person's coat or shirt while neglecting the person within. Pampering the coat or even the shirt of the individual does not reach the person within. He does not feel real pleasure. Similarly, by taking care of the bird cage while neglecting the bird inside is not the way to make the bird happy. This is why people who may be successful, absorbed in material affairs, may still feel empty, unfulfilled, or unsatisfied within. Real happiness is that which touches the soul itself, the true identity of the living being.

The evidence that the soul is inside the body is the consciousness which pervades the body. We find that the best sources for explaining the characteristics of the soul are found in the ancient Vedic literature of India. Many such texts have information about this, but the great classic *Bhagavad-gita* (13.34) explains: "O son of Bharata, as the sun alone illuminates all this universe, so does the living entity, one within the body, illuminate the entire body by consciousness."

Elsewhere in *Bhagavad-gita* Sri Krishna relates the eternal nature of the soul: "Never was there a time when I did not exist, nor you, nor all these kings; nor in the future shall any of us cease to be. As the embodied soul continually passes, in this body, from boyhood to youth to old age, the soul similarly passes into another body at death. The self-realized soul is not bewildered by such a change." (*Bg.*2.12-13)

"Know that which pervades the entire body is indestructible. No one is able to destroy the imperishable soul. Only the material body of the indestructible, immeasurable, and eternal living entity is subject to destruction. (*Bhagavad- Gita*.2.17-18). . . For the soul there is never birth nor death. Nor, having once been, does he ever cease to be. He is unborn, eternal, ever-existing, undying and primeval. He is not slain when the body is slain. (*Bg*.2.20). . . As a person puts on new garments, giving up old ones, similarly, the soul accepts new material bodies, giving up the old and useless ones." (*Bg*. 2.23)

Here in these verses we get great insights into the characteristics and eternal nature of the individual soul. According to these explanations, the soul is completely beyond the influence of the temporary material nature. Furthermore, the size of the soul is also described in the *Svetasvatara Upanishad* (5.9): "When the upper point of a hair is divided into one hundred parts and again each of such parts is further divided into one hundred parts, each such part is the measurement of the dimension of the spirit soul."

According to the *Vedas*, the body is compared to a chariot in which the self is riding. "Transcendentalists who are advanced in knowledge compare the body, which is made by the order of the Supreme Personality of Godhead, to a chariot. The senses are like the horses; the mind, the master of the senses, is like the reins; the objects of the senses are the destinations; intelligence is the chariot driver; consciousness, which spreads throughout the body, is the cause of bondage in this material world." (*Srimad-Bhagavatam* 7.15.41)

The *Katha Upanishad* also explains the refined nature of the soul which makes it so difficult to be seen. It says that within the body, higher than the senses and the sense objects, exists the mind. More subtle than the mind is the intelligence, and higher and more subtle than the intellect is the self. That self is hidden in all beings and does not shine forth, but is seen by subtle seers through their sharp intellect.

Naturally, until our consciousness is cleansed, we recognize various beings according to their body. We may see a person that appears to be a man, a woman, a child, or a baby. Or we may recognize those who appear to be animals, insects, aquatics, or plants. However, once we can see beyond these material bodies, we will see that all these entities are the same. They are all spirit souls.

The *Svetasvatara Upanishad* (5.10-11) states that the self is not man, woman, nor neuter, but appears in different types of bodies only due to previous activities and desires of the living entity. This is how the entity chooses whatever status in which one presently appears. But a person in divine consciousness can perceive that he or she is beyond all designations and activities.

"The humble sage, by virtue of true knowledge, sees with equal vision a learned and gentle *brahmana*, a cow, an elephant, a dog, and a dog-eater (outcaste)." (*Bg.*5.18)

So this is some of the information about the size and nature of the soul as described in the Vedic literature. These verses from the Vedic texts are provided because such details about the soul are not found elsewhere. From this information we can understand that the soul is completely separate from whatever labels or designations we give to the body. This is clearly explained in the following verse from the *Srimad-Bhagavatam*:

"Fatness, thinness, bodily and mental distress, thirst, hunger, fear, disagreement, desires for material happiness, old age, sleep, attachment for material possessions, anger, lamentation, illusion and identification of the body with the self are all transformations of the material covering of the spirit soul. A person absorbed in the material bodily conception is affected by these things, but the soul is free from all bodily conceptions. Consequently, the spirit soul is neither fat nor skinny nor anything else you may consider."

Only in this frame of mind will we be able to reach a stage of peace within ourselves individually and go on to attain peace in the world.

BEING FREE OF ALL DESIGNATIONS

There are two levels of existence; material and spiritual. Designations for the body and mind are material. To be on the spiritual level means to be free from the influence of bodily designations. Neither will you think you are the body, nor will you think that others are their bodies. You will see the individual soul within the body as if seeing a person dressed in clothes.

Our body may be European, or African, American, Christian, or Muslim. But that deals with the body and mind, like the dress or coat of a person. Someone may wear a white shirt and someone else a black or red shirt, but that is not who we are. Nor should it be the basis of our quarrels. If we see only the dress, then we think we are different. If we think we are different and that we oppose each other, then there may be fights or even wars because one side is wearing a white shirt and the other a red shirt. The dress is our covering, it is not the real person. And the dress may even change in color, shape, size, design, and style. Anything material in this world is subject to change. Therefore, we have to look beyond the dress to see the real person within. The spiritual platform is eternal and absolute. Thus, the spiritual being within the covering or dress is the same as every other spiritual being. So where is the reason for fighting?

On the bodily platform we engage in defending our honor and reputation. But what are these? Whatever fame, power, or strength we have clings only to the body. We lose it all when we shed the body at the time of death. The soul is above such things. All material situations are temporary and have nothing to do with the eternal, spiritual self. We are all here in this world for a short time, like travelers on a bus. We have been given a seat or position which we have for a little while. Then we will be forced to give it up at the end of the journey; the end of life. Why, therefore, should we be so attached, so ready to fight, over a temporary seat?

It is obvious that as long as people are in the bodily concept of life, there will not be any real unity or harmony between us. Unity cannot be attained by resolutions, political platforms, social agreements, laws or military actions. It cannot be attained through force. It can only be attained through mutual realization and understanding when we reach the spiritual platform, centered on the fact that we are all spiritual sparks of the Supreme Being. This is the platform of real unity between us. As long as we see our fellow men and women as being merely human, we will continue to suffer disillusionment. Only by seeing the greater potential of the divine nature within all of us, beneath the weakness of the flesh, can we reach unconditional love. Then we can unite in our constitutional position of being eternal servants of the Supreme. That is real unity. Then we are properly centered. Then we can turn to each other with the proper respect and consideration, helping one another and treating each other as we would like to be treated. In such a condition, the whole world works for its own upliftment.

As explained in another of the ancient Vedic texts, the *Sri Isopanishad* (*Mantras* 6-7): "He who sees everything in relation to the Supreme Lord, who sees all entities as His parts and parcels and who sees the Supreme Lord within everything, never hates anything nor any being. One who always sees all living entities as spiritual sparks, in quality one with the Lord, becomes a true knower of things. What, then, can be illusion or anxiety for him?"

CHAPTER FOUR

Seeing the Divinity in Each of Us

Morihei Ueshiba, the founder of the Aikido method of martial arts said: "Above all, one must unite one's heart with that of the gods. The essence of God is love, an all-pervading love that reaches every corner of the universe. If one is not united to God, the universe cannot be harmonized. Martial artists who are not in harmony with the universe are merely executing combat techniques, not Aiki (*Ai*--uniting harmony and love with *ki*--the universal energy)."

This understanding is very important even in ordinary, everyday life. If we are not working in harmony with love and universal energy, we are simply going through daily routines that are ineffectual and empty. We need to practice the methods which also awaken the connection we have with God, the universe, and each other. This is the way we can fully grow and develop. Then our life will have meaning and purpose. We will be guided by our own upliftment and will be able to assist in the upliftment of others. We will be able to recognize the all-pervasiveness of the Supreme Being.

The essence of this perception has been related in the ancient Vedic texts, as we find in the *Svetasvatara Upanishad* (6.11) which states, "He is the one God hidden in all beings, all pervading, the self within all beings, watching over all worlds, dwelling in all beings, the witness, the perceiver." If one can truly understand this and become enlightened in this way, he will see that he is a part of the Supreme Reality and realize his union with all beings. Within that enlightenment one can reach Divine Love. This love is based on the spiritual oneness

39

and harmony between all beings, which is sublime. It is a source of spiritual bliss. It is a love based not on bodily relations or mutual attraction, but it is based on being one in spirit, beyond the temporary nature of the body. This is the love for which everyone searches, from which springs forth peace, harmony, and unity, of which all other kinds of love are mere reflections. This state of being is reached only through spirituality. Therefore, a life without spirituality is a life incomplete. All have the need to fill their souls with spirituality, the presence of God, in order to feel fullness, peace, contentment, and unity.

As the Supreme says in the ancient Vedic text of *Bhagavad-gita* (6.30): "To him who sees Me in everything and everything in Me, I am never lost, and he is not lost to Me."

To begin seeing how things really are, and to recognize the Divinity in each of us, we have to start adjusting our consciousness. This takes place by being trained in spiritual knowledge and by the practice of yoga which purifies the mind. When the mind becomes purified and the false ego no longer influences our vision, we become sensible people. As the *Bhagavad-gita* (13.31-32) says, when a sensible man ceases to see different identities due to different material bodies, he attains the spiritual conception. Those with the vision of eternity see that the soul is transcendental, eternal, and beyond the modes of nature. Despite being within the material body, the soul is above material contact.

As the son is a part and parcel of the father, similarly, we are all individual parts of the supreme spiritual Father. In fact, the whole creation displays different energies which are expansions of the Supreme Energetic. Thus, there is diversity within the variegated material energy which expands from the Supreme Being. These expansions manifest in millions of species of life, as explained in the Vedic literature. Therefore, although we are in different material bodies, we are all expansions of the same spiritual energy. This is oneness and unity in diversity. On the spiritual platform, which is absolute, we are all the same. We are all spiritual beings, servants of the Supreme Being, undergoing life in the material creation. That is real unity. This perception is the perfection of the spiritually conscious person. He sees all living beings as reflections of the One, the Supreme

Being. Thus, in a broad sense, there is one interest. Spiritually there is no clash.

We are all but small reflections of the Supreme Consciousness. When we put the greater whole above ourselves, and realize that we all contribute to the condition of this planet, then uniting with a common cause and with that Supreme Consciousness will be easy.

This planet does not allow us to be isolated. We all must work together and interface with others on some level. One lesson that this school of existence on this planet forces us to learn is that when we come together willingly to communicate, with a positive purpose, or to pray together, and to unite for the good of the whole, then harmony and peace can exist. That peace forms and manifests when we focus on our spiritual nature, which brings between us our unity in the Supreme. Making this the center of our existence will easily bring peace, unity, and harmony in this world because it brings in the spiritual vibration that emanates from the Supreme. That vibration is one of spiritual love. It is all that is eternal. All else is temporary. Therefore, focusing on and using our energy on temporary emotions such as envy, jealousy, and anger, will only keep us far away from the Supreme, and from reaching any peace or unity between us.

We have to recognize how similar we are in order to expand our heart toward others we may have previously rejected. This is how love and understanding can dissolve the boundaries that keep us stifled as a society and individuals, and keep us from entering higher dimensions of consciousness. There is no other way to grow spiritually. A lack of love for each other is a reflection of a lack of love for God.

When we think in spiritual consciousness, we do not recognize others by their differences. We see our similarities. This is easy when we think in terms of being sons and daughters of the same Supreme Father. We all belong to the One. Only in this way can there be universal love among all living entities. Only in this way can we begin to think that we are all related to each other. Once we establish our relationship with the Supreme, then we can establish our true relationship with everyone else. Our spiritual nature is eternal, and our spiritual relation with the Supreme is eternal. Therefore, our spiritual relationship with each other is also eternal. It is not subject to time and circumstances. This central

point has to be established in order for there to be universal peace,
brotherhood, equality, and unity in the world.

In essence, we are all consciousness in material forms. Consciousness
cannot be destroyed. It is the essence of God in each of us. We are all
spiritual beings, reflections of the Divine. We are not our beliefs, our
cultures, or our minds and bodies. We are all divine souls on a
wondrous journey through Truth. We have all manifested from God,
the Supreme Truth, and we are all evolving back to God. As the *Manu-
samhita* (12.125) relates, "Thus, he who by means of Self sees the
self in all created things, after attaining equality with all, enters into
Brahman [spiritual consciousness], the highest place." That is the
ultimate goal.

CHAPTER FIVE

Seeing Our Unity is a Source of Happiness

One of the priorities of human society is that we need to focus on the fundamental unity of human nature and the destiny of humanity. Obviously, the more we see that others are like us, the more fraternity and closeness with others we feel. And that is a source of happiness. Besides, the more people who have the same goals, the more likely those goals will be realized. After all, there is strength in unity. The more unified we are, the more likely mankind can realize its destiny. This is what will naturally bring us all closer together. Once we start functioning together in this way, life will become easier for everyone and social happiness will be an automatic result.

REASONS FOR THE HAPPINESS IN THE VISION OF UNITY

Kindness is a natural virtue in living entities. Kindness to all beings must be the norm, which flourishes and is natural in a society of people who are engaged in devotion to the Supreme. Devotion is the center of life in one who sees that we are all parts of the Supreme. In the mood of devotion to the Divine, that mood becomes friendship and benevolence toward all living beings. Without such devotion, kindness will be restricted or felt only for one's own body and then family. If it expands a little, it will be felt for one's community. If it expands more, it will be felt patriotically, for people living in one's own country, but maybe only of one's own race. If it expands further, the thought of kindness may include all living beings of one's own species. If it expands more, to a truly spiritual perspective, it will include all living beings. But true religionists and those who advocate real kindness must break through all forms of narrow-minded vision and see beyond all bodily distinctions and give up causing any anxiety to any being, and embrace benevolence and mercy for the hearts of all living entities. This is a major step in attaining peace in the world. In such a spiritually conscious atmosphere, people of all lands will respect each other's right to live in peace.

Genuinely moralistic people and real religionists always avoid acts of cruelty. Such acts include those that cause anxiety and suffering, or making agitation or gossip about the bad works of other men and women, or scandalizing and lying about others. It also includes quarreling, saying harsh words, envying the money of others, and wounding them mentally or physically. Then there can be peace.

The purpose of society is to live in peace and harmony so everyone can advance spiritually. With such a proper center in society, there would be a natural harmony, a unity and beauty like the waves in a pond spreading out from a central point after a stone has been thrown into it. That is the beauty that exists when everyone is centered around the eternal nature of the soul, which is to serve the Supreme and to recognize that we are all expansions of the Supreme's energy. However, when others have their own agendas, their own desires, different interests and goals of life, then everyone wants to throw a stone into the pond. What happens then is that all the waves spreading out crash into each other, causing chaos, friction, and then quarrels, fights, and wars. This is what we have today. Everyone's ideas interfering with others. Thus, there is no peace in society, no unity, no harmony. However, with spiritual consciousness, a person ceases being envious of others, and redirects his energy from trying to satisfy all of their material and sensual desires. When we are no longer envious and can see each other as parts of the Supreme, then there will be real peace, unity, and brotherhood in society.

When we break through the barriers that separate us, then we can understand that the supreme friend, proprietor, master, and lover, is the Supreme Being. So the Supreme Being is the ultimate object of our loving propensities. This is Divine Love. When we all direct our love toward the Supreme, rising above the differences in religions or the way we express that love, then immediately universal love, unity, and tranquillity will manifest. Just as when we water the root of the tree, all of the branches, twigs, leaves, and flowers become nourished. When we see each other in this form of universal brotherhood, all connected with the Supreme Being in the same way that the leaves and flowers are connected to the tree, there is a natural happiness that comes from seeing each other in this way. It provides a means to see each other as parts of the Supreme. It is in this way that we are all truly related. When we reach a stage of spiritual happiness because of rising above the bodily platform, then we will see that we are all spiritually connected.

This vision is also a cause of supreme spiritual happiness, and it is natural to want to share this vision or consciousness with others. The more who share this vision and realization about our real identity, the more powerful it becomes and the more it spreads to others. As it is related in the *Bhagavad-gita* (9.2): "This knowledge is the king of education, the most secret of all secrets. It is the purest knowledge, and because it gives direct perception of the self by realization, it is the perfection of religion. It is everlasting, and it is joyfully performed."

We have to understand that we are all spiritual beings who have somehow come into this temporary material world. We are all wearing these temporary material bodies. The purpose of this human form of life is to regain our spiritual position, so let us all help each other to do that. That is universal brotherhood and spiritual unity. As Sri Krishna states in *Bhagavad-gita* (4.35): "And when you have thus learned the truth, you will know that all living beings are but part of Me--and that they are in Me, and are Mine."

ATTAINING PEACE ON THE PLANET

Everyone in this world wants peace and happiness. The problem is that in this material world many people want the peace and beautiful conditions of heaven but without God. That is not possible. The basis of a peaceful planet starts with peace in the minds of the individuals who live on the planet. And the basis of individual peace begins with understanding our spiritual identity and connection with the Supreme. As it states in *Bhagavad-gita* (2.66): "One who is not connected with the Supreme can have neither transcendental intelligence nor a steady mind, without which there is no possibility of peace. And how can there be happiness without peace?"

So the most important thing to do then is to help provide the genuine spiritual knowledge that allows people to understand their true spiritual identity, which is beyond the national, cultural, or even conventional religious designations. The *Bhagavad-gita* (4.39) states: "A faithful man who is dedicated to transcendental knowledge and who subdues his senses is eligible to achieve such knowledge, and having achieved it he quickly attains the supreme spiritual peace."

God holds the supreme peace. Connecting with God lets us share in that supreme peace. We must fill our hearts with the presence of God, after which we will be able to radiate our love equally to all people. When we are able to see the Self in all people, we will be able to spread that love in all directions as an act of devotion. In that consciousness we will see that everything and everyone is a part of the energy of the Supreme. Therein is the potential for real peace, which will come when each of us realizes that we are all equal aspects of the Supreme Being. Then we will be able to work together in harmony.

ACHIEVING PEACE AND HAPPINESS
FOR THE INDIVIDUAL AND THE WORLD

The purpose of life is really quite simple: Life is meant for being happy. But real happiness, which exists on the spiritual platform, is always steady and, in fact, continually increasing according to one's spiritual advancement. Such persons who understand their spiritual identity and are self-satisfied and content within themselves find happiness everywhere.

The *Katha Upanishad* (2.5.12-13) says that to those who have realized their self and see the Supreme Being residing within their heart and in all beings as the Superself, belong eternal happiness and eternal peace; but not to others.

The original spiritual form of the living being is *sac-cid-ananda*: eternal, full of knowledge and bliss. The living being's spiritual form is never limited by the material body or one's situation. The only limiting factor is the living being's consciousness or lack of spiritual awareness. When the living entity regains his original spiritual consciousness, realizing he is not the body, he naturally feels very happy and jolly, being freed from the limited and temporary perspective one has while being controlled by the illusory, material energy. He also understands that this material world is not his real home, and it has nothing substantial to offer him since real pleasure and happiness actually come from within on the spiritual level. As stated in *Bhagavad-gita* by Sri Krishna: "One who is thus transcendentally situated at once realizes the Supreme Brahman and becomes fully joyful. He never laments nor desires to have anything; he is equally disposed to every living entity." (*Bhagavad-Gita*.18.54)

As one attains spiritual vision, he becomes completely free from illusion, anxiety, anger, and hatred. This freedom is felt in a natural joy that comes from realizing one's eternal, spiritual identity. But this freedom is attained to its fullest extent when one is released from all material limitations and is independent to express one's love and happiness in the unbounded loving relationship between the finite living being and the infinite Supreme Lord. It is this experience and knowledge which is the ultimate uniting factor between all living entities. In this way, we are certainly all brothers and sisters, being sons and daughters of the same Supreme Father. Without this vision we simply remain like uncivilized, quarreling animals. Therefore, it is obvious that to see the difference between the body and soul, and to recognize the qualitative spiritual oneness among us all, are absolutely necessary if we expect to establish real peace and unity in the world.

THE NEED FOR GOOD LEADERS AND RULERS

A godless civilization creates a hellish world. Such a civilization increases material desires, and the conditions of life become intolerable. If the leaders are also godless and foolish, they will try to devise plans to arrange for peace in the world according to materialistic considerations. These frequently evolve around political and economic adjustments. Because such attempts are themselves temporary and illusory, failing to produce the anticipated results, the people continue to elect other blind and incompetent leaders, one after another, in the hopes of finding one who can arrange the world the way they wish, for peace and prosperity. Though such leaders make loud, confident promises that conditions will improve, they are incapable of offering real solutions.

There is a great need in society for strong, spiritually educated leaders. Without the vigilance of a strong ruler, impious and wicked men will gain control in an attempt to push their cause and fulfill their desires. Consequently, all social order will disappear, taking away all hopes of peace.

Unless thieves, rapists, killers, and other criminals in the land are afraid of the punishments that will be inflicted on them by the head of state who rules with strength, there will not be any peace or prosperity in the country. Criminals flourish because of the cowardly nature of the executive heads of state. But when they rule in a strong manner, miscreants cannot prosper. Therefore, leaders must impose strict measures against criminals who refuse to help maintain a peaceful society and try to harm and take advantage of honest citizens. The prime duty of a leader is to make sure that peaceful, law-abiding citizens are protected. That brings peace in the state.

Leaders must keep in mind the basic human rights of all people and act as caretakers of others rather than thinking he or she is a proprietor of a certain district or country. In order to be effective in this age, leaders must see the presence of God in everyone. In this way, a leader can act as a representative of the Supreme Will. Acting in this strong but loving disposition, all who work with such leaders can also receive and help transmit this love to others.

Leaders who take their position while feeling love for their people will more likely establish policies that will truly benefit all beings. When people see this in their leaders and feel cared for, they will feel more secure and will readily reciprocate and cooperate with their leaders and show support. A bad king or ruler spoils the kingdom, while the whole world can be united and peaceful under proper leadership. A good population under proper leadership is the basic principle for peace, prosperity, and spiritual progress.

CHAPTER SIX

What We Need To Begin Working Together

STARTING WITH THE BASICS

When it comes to working together, there are many things that we could be doing. However, let us face the fact that we are a long way from establishing peace and spiritual harmony on the planet. Thus, in paving the way in which we can start working toward world peace and bringing unity between us, we have to start with the basics.

One of the first things we need to do is start taking a new look at each other. And while we do that, let us also put aside our prejudices and look at the ways we can improve ourselves rather than at the faults of everyone else. As it is explained in the *Dhammapada*, an ancient Chinese text, "To see another's fault is easy; to see one's own is hard. Men winnow the faults of others like chaff; their own they hide as a crafty gambler hides a losing throw." (*Dhammapada* 252)

Furthermore, *Ephesians* (4.31-2) explains how we must also set aside our anger and ill-feelings in order to come together, and be forgiving toward one another. "Let all bitterness, and wrath, and anger, and clamour, and evil-speaking, be put away from you, with all malice. And be kind to one another, tender-hearted, forgiving one another, even as God for Christ's sake hath forgiven you."

In this way, let us also focus on our similarities, the common principles of our religions, and the harmony and peace we could have if we worked together for the collective good.

The Buddhist *Sutta-Nipata* (148) explains that, "As a mother, even at the risk of her own life, protects her son; so let him that has recognized the truth cultivate good will without measure amongst all beings." Through this means we can reach a stage of appreciation and respect for all beings; an understanding that all life is precious. This in itself is a means to happiness, as related in the *Dammapada* (39), "Full of love for all things in the world, practicing virtue in order to benefit others, this man alone is happy."

THE GOLDEN RULE IS UNIVERSAL

The idea of practicing virtue to help and respect others is not absent from any part of the world. It is a basic law found everywhere. Therefore, no one has an excuse to not follow it. If we ever expect to have peace in the world, this is certainly where we can begin.

The importance of this was well stated by Mohandas Gandhi: "To injure a single human being is to injure those divine powers within us, and thus the harm reaches not only that one human being, but with him the whole world."

This makes it clear that whatever disrespect or harm we show to others (providing they have no criminal intent) is not isolated, but has its effects far and wide, and can do as much inner harm to us as we do to others. In other words, by following the Golden Rule we help oursleves as much as those we meet.

One of the earliest references to the Golden Rule is found in India in the *Mahabharata* (13.5571), which states, "This is the sum of all true righteousness--Treat others as thou would'st thyself be treated. Do nothing to thy neighbor, which hereafter thou would'st not have thy neighbor do to thee. In causing pleasure or in giving pain, in doing good or injury to others, in granting or refusing a request, a man obtains a proper rule of action by looking on his neighbor as himself."

The *Manu-samhita* (2.161) also explains, "Wound not others, do no one injury by thought or deed, utter no word to pain thy fellow creatures."

From the Middle-east, in Judaism we find in the *Talmud*, "What is hurtful to yourself do not to your fellow man. That is the Torah and

the remainder is but commentary. Go learn it." *Leviticus* (19.17-18)
explains, "Thou shalt not hate thy brother in thine heart. . . Thou shalt
not avenge, nor bear any grudge. . . but thou shalt love thy neighbor
as thyself."

Similar expressions are found amongst the Christians in *Matthew*
(7.12) and *Luke* (6.31) which explain, "All things whatsoever ye
would that men should do to you, do ye even so to them; for this is
the law and the prophets."

I Thessalonians (5.15) states, "See that none render evil for evil
unto any man; but ever follow that which is good, both among
yourselves, and to all men." And *Hebrews* (13.1) says: "Let brotherly
love continue. Be not forgetful to entertain strangers; for thereby
some have entertained angels unawares."

The most important of all Christian principles is found in *Matthew*
(22.37-40): "Thou shalt love the Lord thy God with all thy heart, and
with all thy soul, and with all thy mind. This is the first and great
commandment, and the second is like unto it, thou shalt love thy
neighbor as thyself. On these two commandments hang all the law and
the prophets."

Furthermore, the words of Jesus explain in *John* (13.34-5): "A
new commandment I give unto you, that ye love one another as I have
loved you, that ye also love one another. By this shall all men know
that ye are my disciples, if ye have love one to another."

From the Orient, in the *Analects* (15.23) of Confucianism, it
states, "Tzu Kung asked saying: Is there any one maxim which ought
to be acted upon throughout one's whole life? The Master replied:
Surely the maxim of reciprocity is such: Do not unto others what you
would not they should do unto you."

Also in the *Analects* (6.28) we find, "The man of moral virtue,
wishing to stand firm himself, will lend firmness unto others; wishing
himself to be enlightened, he will enlighten others. To be able to do to
others as we would be done by--this is the true domain of moral
virtue."

In the Jain religion we find more references to the Golden Rule.
In the *Yogashastra* (2.20) it states, "In happiness and suffering, in joy
and grief, regard all creatures as you regard your own self, and do not

injure others with that which would injure yourself." Also (2.37), "Viler than unbelievers are those cruel ones who make the law that teaches killing."

In Buddhism, the *Udanavarya* (5.18) simply states, "Hurt not others with that which pains yourself."

In the *Masnavi* of Islam it is said, "If every one saw his own faults first, how should he be neglectful of correcting himself. These people are thoughtless as to, and unacquainted with themselves; and consequently they speak of the faults of one another."

So in every part of the world and in every religion there are references relating the need to respect one another and treat others as you would like to be treated. What a difference there would be in the world if everyone immediately began to practice what they preach from their own doctrine.

GOOD RULES FOR LIFE

A good standard of morals must be followed because such rules promote the prosperity of social life. If a standard of morals is not followed, then the lack of respect people will have for each other, and the crimes that follow, will force all social happiness to quickly disappear. Therefore, we should cultivate the principle sentiments of love, kindness, friendship, and mercy, for the promotion of social good and prosperity. Then the evil propensities--envy, malice, anger, and greed--will not be so apt to enter our minds and pollute society. The point is, universal love is universal pleasure. Therefore, we must adopt such means to promote this social good.

However, higher than developing simple moralistic principles is developing faith in the Supreme Being. Good moral values will be there automatically with faith in the Supreme, which increases the propensity for virtue on earth.

The *Manu-samhita* (6.92) also supplies some good rules for which to live: "Contentment, patience under injury, self-subjugation, honesty, restraint of all the sensual organs, purity, devotion, knowledge of the Deity (God), veracity, and abstinence from anger, these form the tenfold summary of duty."

This is very similar to what is stated in the Jain scripture, *Purushartha Siddyupaya* (204): "Forgiveness, humility, straightforwardness, truth, contentment, restraint, austerities, charity, non-attachment, and chastity are the ten observances to be followed."

All moralistic rules point toward a life of simple living and high thinking. This provides the means by which we all can evolve to a higher level of being and a loftier state of consciousness. This is the way we can always live peacefully with the intent of making spiritual advancement. We must always remember that we are transients in this world and must prepare to reach our real home in the next world. Therefore, do your duties and cultivate devotion to God as a means to obtain the proper end of life. Lead a pure life, avoid sins, and do as much good as you can to your fellow man. Be humble, live simply, be tolerant, and bear your difficulties heroically. Do not brag of your good deeds or accomplishments, and treat everyone with proper respect. Do everything for spiritual cultivation, which is really the ultimate purpose of life. Never do anything which will displease the Supreme, and have a strong faith that He will look after you, especially when you leave this world.

Always remember that spiritually all men, women, and all living entities are brothers and sisters. The business of dividing into camps of friends and enemies due to bodily conceptions has little to do with spiritual reality. As the Bible says, "There is neither Jew nor Greek, there is neither bond nor free, there is neither male nor female: for ye are all one. . . " (*Galatians* 3.28) This is our common ground, and must be our central focus.

So instead of focusing on differences, we can easily develop unity by concentrating on our similarities. Common principles of all religions and cultures that we can practice together include: Never hurt the feelings of others. Speak the truth. Do not kill any sentient beings. Cultivate the virtues of humility, courage, forgiveness, tolerance, and compassion. Love all, be kind to all. Be good, and do good. Be charitable. Purify the heart. Serve humanity. Share what you have with others. Love thy neighbor as thyself. This is the essence of all religions.

Ashoka's Edicts also explains in which activities the essence of religion exists. "Wherein does religion consist? It consists in doing as little harm as possible, in doing good in abundance, in the practice of love, compassion, of truthfulness and purity, in all walks of life."

James (1.27) mentions taking care of the poor and destitute. "Pure religion and undefiled before God and the father is this, to visit the fatherless and widows in their affliction, and to keep himself unspotted from the world." Furthermore, "In as much as you have done it unto one of the least of these my brethren, ye have done it unto me." (Matthew 25.40) And in the end, God will reward everyone accordingly: "God will render to every man according to his deeds." (Romans 2.6)

As you continue to grow spiritually, you will perceive your progress toward inner peace by the following symptoms, the lack of which shows those who still have much progress to make:

1. The tendency to think and act deliberately, rather than from fears based on past experiences or fear-based beliefs that have been passed down to you.
2. An unmistakable ability to enjoy each moment.
3. A loss of interest in judging others.
4. A loss of interest in judging self, except for the level of your spiritual progress.
5. A loss of interest in conflict.
6. A loss of interest in interpreting the actions of others.
7. A loss of ability to worry.
8. Frequent, overwhelming episodes of appreciation.
9. Contented feelings of connectedness with the Supreme, others, and nature.
10. Frequent attacks of smiling through the heart.
11. Increasing receptiveness to kindness, and uncontrollable urges to reciprocate.
12. An increasing tendency to allow things to unfold rather than resisting and manipulating.

Higher still is the supreme goal of life, as mentioned in the Vedic texts such as the following: "Now [that you have this human form], therefore, you should inquire into Brahman [the spiritual, Absolute Truth]." (*Vedanta-sutras* 1.1.1) Inquiring into the nature of the Absolute Truth and our real, spiritual identity is the highest level of human evolutionary development.

Therefore, "Do not stay in illusion, go to the eternal reality. Do not stay in darkness, go to the light. Do not keep taking material bodies, become immortal." (*Brihadaranyaka Upanishad* 1.3.28) And, as stated by Suta Gosvami, "Life's desires should never be directed towards sense gratification. One should desire only a healthy life, or self-preservation, since a human being is meant for inquiring about the Absolute Truth. Nothing else should be the goal of one's works." (*Srimad-Bhagavatam* 1.2.10) Indeed, learning about, understanding, and realizing one's real spiritual identity is the ultimate position in life. In this purified consciousness one can enter the spiritual realm and attain the highest state of peace and happiness. Those who have attained this state of consciousness can be a guiding hand to help show others the way to see the unity between us all.

Conclusion

Two factors that keep the world from being united is the presumption of racial superiority, and the desire to conquer and convert. The only way to breakthrough the barriers of distinction that seem to exist between us is with love. However, that love cannot be love of the body or society. It has to be better and higher than that. It has to be a spiritual love for all beings. The *Dammapada* (5-6) explains: "For hatred does not cease by hatred at any time: hatred ceases by love, this is an old rule. The world does not know that we must all come to an end here; but those who know it, their quarrels cease at once."

Being on this planet is similar to being on a plane going from one place to another. We are all transients sharing a flight, which is temporary. We may not have the best seats for the moment, but we will soon be landing somewhere else. So why should we engage in quarreling over temporary seats? Furthermore, those who have the best seats--fancy houses and high paying jobs--will also have to give up their seats when the flight is over, at the time of death. And where they will go after that, no one can know for sure. Therefore, those who understand the temporary nature of this world will stop fighting and help one another to get through this life on earth. We must be willing to encourage, not threaten life.

Our prejudices restrict our ability to progress individually and socially. Spiritual understanding and enlightenment, ultimately, is all that will allow us to grow beyond our prejudices and living in a world of distinctions, and bring us to a world of peace and unity.

Prejudice is more than a conflict with others, it is an internal fight, a negative activity within yourself. You carry it with you wherever you go. This is, of course, a sign of great immaturity. It is natural that as people mature, and especially if they develop spiritually, they will get tired of this fight. Only people who never grow or fully develop hold onto their immature ways, such as maintaining their own internal struggles and outward fights over their prejudices. It is a pity because they never see beyond that; never seeing the true potential, the spiritual nature, of others. Thus, this lack of maturity in their perception wears them down and stifles their ability to contribute to society and themselves. They always remain retarded in this sense and never reach their full potential. As you mature in life, as you develop spiritually, the fight over prejudicial distinctions becomes boring. It is a waste of time. It is beneath your dignity.

This is accomplished through the participation of real religion, which is to rise above the dictates of the mind and senses and to see the Divinity, the Supersoul, within everybody with Divine Love. Real religion means to develop love of God. Such love naturally includes all of the parts and parcels of God, all the spirit souls. Real religion means shedding the differences between the names and forms of the Divine, and to work together for a Universal Brotherhood.

You can look at any country where society is divided by prejudicial quarrels--racial and cultural conflict, or tribalism--and recognize how they are prevented from developing as a nation because so much energy is diverted toward the quarrels, or fighting and killing. No such country or community can call themselves civilized when they reflect this kind of animal consciousness. They will certainly not contribute much to the progress of their people or others in the world.

When you have more energy to devote to love, acceptance, peace, and harmony, you automatically have less energy to extend toward anger, hate and prejudicial fighting. Prejudicial anger arises from a person who thinks the source of his or her problems or pleasures are other human beings. However, the more you can see that your source of pleasure is actually your higher self, or your spiritual being, you naturally feel less dependent on the world and the people in it. You also feel less frustration. You then see that you are also a co-creator of your life. You have independence to decide your future and the life you wish to lead. It is up to you to change things if you wish. Then you will be more likely to receive the energies of grace, peace, forgiveness, and understanding of yourself and others, and more freedom. This can bring the end of hatred and intolerance.

One thing that should be obvious from the information that has been presented in this book is that the main cause for the increase in disease, crime, poverty, and despair in humanity, is forgetfulness of our divine nature and neglect of our spiritual purpose. When so much human energy no longer has to be exerted toward self-protection and to gratifying the desires of the mind and senses, it can be directed toward our future development and peaceful coexistence. Love, spiritual love from the Supreme Creator, makes this world beautiful. It is the selfishness and hatred in mankind that causes all the trouble.

It will be those people who have evolved in their own consciousness to the point where they have a greater unity with the oneness of everything and the Supreme who will be able to have and promote unity between us all and peace in the world. Such people will be, and are, the true peacekeepers in the world; not the politicians who are trying to divide or fashion the world in a way that is pleasing only to certain political interests. Such material changes simply give way to the need to make more changes. They never last. The world is meant for a higher, more progressive state of existence and cooperation. If we do not achieve this, then what have we accomplished? Focusing on our similarities is easier than attending to our differences. It is also a positive action. Concentrating our minds on what is positive brings positivity into the world, which also creates an uplifting future. Only through the development of our spiritual consciousness will there be the way for true peace, harmony, and unity in the world.

References

Abundant Peace:The Biography of Morihei Ueshiba Founder of Aikido,
 by John Stevens, Shambala Publications, 1987
Bhagavad-gita As It Is, translated by A. C. Bhaktivedanta Swami,
 Bhaktivedanta Book Trust, New York/Los Angeles, 1972
Bible, New York International Bible Society, 1981
Book of Morman, The Church of Jesus Christ of Latter-day Saints, Salt
 Lake City, Utah, 1976
The Holy Quran, 'Abdullah Yusaf 'Ali, Amana Corporation, Brentwood,
 Maryland, 1989
Mahabharata, translated by C. Rajagopalachari, Bharatiya Vidya
 Bhavan, New Delhi, 1972
Mahabharata, Kamala Subramaniam, Bharatiya Vidya Bhavan, Bombay,
 1982
The Law of Manu, [*Manu-samhita*], translated by Georg Buhlerg, Motilal
 Banarsidass, Delhi, 1970
The Secret Teachings of the Vedas, by Stephen Knapp
Sri Isopanisad, translated by A. C. Bhaktivedanta Swami, Bhaktivedanta Book
 Trust, New York/Los Angeles, 1969
Srimad-Bhagavatam, translated by A. C. Bhaktivedanta Swami,
 Bhaktivedanta Book trust, New York/Los Angeles, 1972
Twelve Essential Upanishads, Tridandi Sri Bhakti Prajnan Yati, Sree
 Gaudiya Math, Madras, 1982. Includes the *Isha, Kena, Katha, Prashna,
 Mundaka, Mandukya, Taittiriya, Aitareya, Chandogya, Brihadaranyaka,
 Svetasvatara,* and *Gopalatapani Upanishad* of the Pippalada section of the
 Atharva-veda.
The Universal Path to Enlightenment, by Stephen Knapp
Vishnu Purana, translated by H. H. Wilson, Nag Publishers, Delhi

ABBREVIATIONS

Bhagavad-gita is abbreviated in this book as *Bg.*
Manu-samhita is *Manu.*
Srimad-Bhagavatam or *Bhagavat Purana* is *Bhag.*

ABOUT THE AUTHOR

Stephen Knapp grew up in a Christian family, during which time he seriously studied the Bible to understand its teachings. In his late teenage years, however, he sought answers to questions not easily explained in Christian theology. So he began to search through other religions and philosophies from around the world and started to find the answers for which he was looking. He also studied a variety of occult sciences, ancient mythology, mysticism, yoga, and the spiritual teachings of the East. After his first reading of the *Bhagavad-gita*, he felt he had found the last piece of the puzzle he had been putting together through all of his research. Therefore, he continued to study all of the major Vedic texts of India to gain a better understanding of the Vedic science.

It is known amongst all Eastern mystics that anyone, regardless of qualifications, academic or otherwise, who does not engage in the spiritual practices described in the Vedic texts, cannot actually enter into understanding the depths of the Vedic spiritual science, nor acquire the realizations that should accompany it. So, rather than pursuing his research in an academic atmosphere at a university, Stephen directly engaged in the spiritual disciplines that have been recommended for hundreds of years. He continued his study of Vedic knowledge and spiritual practice under the guidance of a spiritual master. Through this process, and with the sanction of His Divine Grace A. C. Bhaktivedanta Swami Prabhupada, he became initiated into the genuine and authorized spiritual line of the Brahma-Madhava-Gaudiya *sampradaya*, which is a disciplic succession that descends back through Sri Caitanya Mahaprabhu and Sri Vyasadeva, the compiler of Vedic literature, and further back to Sri Krishna. Besides being *brahminically* initiated, Stephen has also been to India several times and traveled extensively throughout the country, visiting most of the major holy places and gaining a wide variety of spiritual experiences that only such places can give.

Stephen has been writing *The Eastern Answers to the Mysteries of Life* series, which so far includes *The Secret Teachings of the Vedas*, *The Universal Path to Enlightenment*, and *The Vedic Prophecies: A New Look into the Future*. He has also written a novel, *Destined for Infinity*, for those who prefer lighter reading, or learning spiritual knowledge in the context of a spiritual adventure. Stephen has put the culmination of over twenty-five years of continuous research and travel experience into his books in an effort to share it with those who are also looking for higher levels of spiritual understanding.

61

If you have enjoyed this book, or if you are serious about finding higher levels of real spiritual Truth, you will also want to get:

The Secret Teachings of the Vedas

This book presents the essence of the ancient Eastern philosophy and summarizes some of the most elevated and important of all spiritual knowledge. This enlightening information is explained in a clear and concise way and is essential for all who want to increase their spiritual understanding, regardless of what their religious background may be. If you are looking for a book to give you an in-depth introduction to the Vedic spiritual knowledge, and to get you started in real spiritual understanding, this is the book!

The topics include: What is your real spiritual identity; the Vedic explanation of the soul; scientific evidence that consciousness is separate from but interacts with the body; the real unity between us all; how to attain the highest happiness and freedom from the cause of suffering; the law of karma and reincarnation; the karma of a nation; where you are really going in life; the real process of progressive evolution; life after death--heaven, hell, or beyond; a description of the spiritual realm; the nature of the Absolute Truth--personal God or impersonal force; recognizing the existence of the Supreme; the reason why we exist at all; and much more. This book provides the answers to questions not found in other religions or philosophies, and condenses information from a wide variety of sources that would take a person years to assemble. It also contains many quotations from the Vedic texts to let the texts speak for themselves, and to show the knowledge the Vedas have held for thousands of years. It also explains the history and origins of the Vedic literature. This book has been called one of the best reviews of Eastern philosophy available.

There is also a special section on traveling to the major historical holy sites of South India with over 75 photographs of art work, sculptures, deities, architecture, and some of the most amazing temples you will see anywhere. This section elaborates on the many ancient legends connected with these important places and what it is like to travel and see them today.

To get your copy, order it from your local bookstore (ISBN:0-9617410-1-5), or simply send $14.95, plus $2.50 for postage and handling ($7.50 for overseas orders) to:

The World Relief Network, P. O. Box 15082, Detroit, Michigan, 48215-0082, U. S. A.

Much rare information is also found in Volume Two of this series:

The Universal Path to Enlightenment

Although all religions and spiritual processes are meant to lead you toward enlightenment, they are not all the same in regard to the methods they teach, nor in the level of philosophical understanding they offer. So an intelligent person will make comparisons between them to understand the aims and distinctions of each religion, and which may give the most complete philosophy. This book presents a most interesting and revealing survey of the major spiritual paths of the world and describes their origins, histories, philosophical basis, and goals. This book will help you decide which path may give you the highest levels of spiritual understanding, and to see the similarities between all religions.

You Will Discover

--the essential similarities of all religions that all people of any culture can practice, which would bring about a united world religion, or "THE UNIVERSAL PATH TO ENLIGHTENMENT."

--how Christianity and Judaism were greatly influenced by the early "pagan" religions and adopted many of their legends, holidays, and rituals that are still practiced today.

--about evidence that shows Jesus may have traveled to the East and learned its spiritual knowledge, and then made bhakti-yoga the essence of his teachings.

--who were the real Vedic Aryans, the founders of the earliest of religions and organized cultures, and how widespread and influential their civilization was to other cultures, such as Egyptian, Greek, Oriental, etc., and how their Vedic teachings are still found in Christianity and other traditions today, which makes them the source of the world's spiritual heritage.

--the philosophical basis and origin of Christianity, Judaism, Islam, Hinduism, Buddhism, Zoroastrianism, Jainism, Sikhism, and many others.

--about the different yoga systems, such as raja-yoga, hatha-yoga, bhakti-yoga, mantra-yoga, etc., what their goals are, and how practical they are in this age.

--about the different mystic powers and experiences that can be attained through yoga.

--what the qualifications are of a genuine spiritual teacher.

--the bliss and results of attaining spiritual enlightenment or experiencing the Absolute.

--and, most importantly, what is the real purpose of a spiritual path that you should strive for, and how to practice the path that is especially recommended as the easiest and most effective for the people of this age to attain real spiritual enlightenment.

--and much more information not easily found elsewhere.

There is also a special section on seeing spiritual India. You will tour the famous temples and holy places of Eastern India, from Madras in the South to New Delhi in the North. You will learn about some of the most important and sacred temples and towns in the world where several of the major religions originated. Almost 100 photographs are included of a variety of temples, holy sites, art, sculptures, and people engaged in all aspects of life in India and Nepal. A great adventure and reference for those who want to travel in this area.

To get your copy, see your local book store to order it (ISBN 0-9617410-2-3), or simply send $14.95, plus $2.50 for postage and handling ($7.50 for overseas orders) to: The World Relief Network, P. O. Box 15082, Detroit, Michigan, 48215-0082, U. S. A.

The Vedic Prophecies:
A New Look into the Future

The Vedic prophecies take you to the end of time! This is the first book ever to present the unique predictions found in the ancient Vedic texts of India. These prophecies are like no others and will provide you with a very different view of the future and how things fit together in the plan for the universe. These prophecies will surprise you.

Now you can discover the amazing secrets that are hidden in the oldest spiritual writings on the planet. Find out what they say about the distant future, and what the seers of long ago saw in their visions of the destiny of the world.

This book will reveal predictions of deteriorating social changes and how to avoid them; future droughts and famines; low-class rulers and evil governments; whether there will be another appearance (second coming) of God; and predictions of a new spiritual awareness and how it will spread around the world. You will also learn the answers to such questions as:

- Does the future get worse or better?
- Will there be future world wars or global disasters?
- What lies beyond the predictions of Nostradamus, the Mayan prophecies, or the Biblical apocalypse?
- Are we in the end times? How to recognize them if we are.
- Does the world come to an end? If so, when and how?

Now you can find out what the future holds. The Vedic Prophecies carry an important message and warning for all humanity, which needs to be understood now!

There is also a special section on seeing spiritual India. This takes you through the famous temples and holy places of Western India, from Jaipur in Central India all the way to Bangalore in the South. Now you can tour them through their histories, legends, and miraculous stories, along with over 65 photographs of temples, holy sites, art, sculptures, sages and people of India. A wonderful addition!

To get your copy, order it from your bookstore (ISBN:0-9617410-4-X) or simply send $14.95 plus $2.50 for postage and handling ($3.50 for Canada, or $7.50 for overseas orders) to: The World Relief Network, P.O.Box 15082, Detroit, Michigan, 48215-0082, U.S.A.